T0090651

PROOF GOD HEARS YOUR PRAYERS

A True Story of How God Made the Impossible Possible

Jennifer Crouse

Cover Image by Dustin Crouse

WestBow Press books may be ordered through booksellers or by contacting:

WestBow Press
A Division of Thomas Nelson & Zondervan
1663 Liberty Drive
Bloomington, IN 47403
www.westbowpress.com
1 (866) 928-1240

ISBN: 978-1-5127-2047-1 (sc)
ISBN: 978-1-5127-2048-8 (e)

Library of Congress Control Number: 2015918908

Print information available on the last page.

WestBow Press rev. date: 11/13/2015

Contents

Acknowledgements

God has placed a number of amazing people in my life and He has always had perfect timing. While I was writing this book God continued to provide me with the support I needed and that was through my good friend, Beth Davis. I would like to thank Beth for all of the support she provided me during the writing of this book. Beth helped me to believe that I could fulfill my dream of being an Author. Beth was also my editor and I feel blessed to have shared this writing journey with my special friend. Finally, I would like to thank all of my friends and family that have helped me through my tragedy and helped me to find my *purpose* in my life.

Introduction

Prayer has always been a big part of my life and an act that I never thought twice about doing. One of my first childhood memories is kneeling next to my bed to pray before I went to sleep. I specifically remember my mother kneeling next to me with my brothers, Hubert Jr. and Raymond, as she taught us how to pray. It soon provided me with a sense of security. Even as a child I knew that God could hear my prayers and He was not only God, but my best friend.

As I wrote this book, I recalled several memories throughout my life of times I spent in prayer. Some of them were times of sorrow, some fear, some happiness and some of thankfulness for God's blessings. I have decided to open my heart and share these stories of prayer with each person who reads this book. I believe I have been called to share my undeniable belief that God hears our prayers. I *know* God saved my life to be a testimony to others and prove that through prayer the impossible *can* become possible.

CHAPTER 1

A Flashback to My Childhood

Beep….Beep…..Beep……

"What is that noise?" I strained as I attempted to open my eyes, but all I could do was squint. "Why will my eyes not open?" was the second question I asked myself as I struggled to look at the white walls in front of me. I appeared to be floating as I noticed my body was slowly moving from side to side. I attempted to call out, "Mom, Dad, Hubert, Raymond?", but I could not move my mouth. Then I heard voices…..I could vaguely see a tall man in a white coat and a woman standing beside him in blue nursing scrubs entering this white room.

"How old is she?" said the man in a serious deep voice.

"She is 16. She was flown here from a small town south of us" said the woman.

The male voice then said, "Any family?"

"Yes, her parents are waiting to speak with you" the woman replied.

Yes, I was only 16 years old at the time. The small town the medical staff was talking about was Walsenburg, Colorado where I lived in the country with my parents, Hubert Sr. and Marlene Aguirre. I had two loving and protective brothers, Hubert Jr. and Raymond. We moved to this property in the country when I was five years old and I was not happy about the move to say the least. My first home was a big two-story home on a large beautiful ranch where my father raised many cattle. Unfortunately, the price of beef dropped quickly one year and we lost the ranch. These types of things are very difficult for a five year-old to fully understand. All I knew was that I was sadly leaving my kindergarten friends and moving to a much smaller home.

I will never forget the drive to our new home. It was winter and cold; the old International truck we were in was one of my father's work trucks that did not have much of a heater. I remember thinking, "Why are we in *this* truck? Where is our new truck?" Of course now I understand everything had been repossessed by the bank, but at the age of 5 it was impossible to comprehend. I felt indescribably sad and worst of all I could see the sadness in my parent's eyes.

When we arrived at our new home I could not believe how old it looked. It was a small white farm home with three bedrooms and one bathroom. All the rooms were very small and the house was heated by a fireplace that appeared it could fall apart at any time. I remember looking over at a strange black structure in the kitchen and I asked my mother, "What is that?" She replied, "That is a woodstove, it is where we will be doing our cooking." This was shocking to me. I couldn't believe we would have to start a fire just to make our food. I then learned the water to our home came from a well and the well water was not safe to drink. We would have to haul our drinking water from a local gas station every day.

As my mother helped my brothers and I get ready for bed that night she discovered the back rooms were too cold to sleep in and quickly informed us we would be sleeping in the living room next to the fireplace. This was the highlight of the day! We were never allowed to sleep in the living room before. It became more like a slumber party to me. My sadness turned into joy and I found myself liking the home more and more.

Even though we did not have a bed to kneel next to that night, my mother still led us in our bedtime prayer. I could tell her heart was heavy that night as she prayed. I could only imagine how sad she felt knowing the luxuries she had and seeing the challenges she would now face with this home. But as we prayed that night, I knew God was going to take care of my family. God had provided me with my very own slumber party and that was all the confirmation I needed to know that this home would be blessed.

Over the next couple of days my family adjusted to our new home and it did not seem as bad as it first appeared. That Sunday night I was excited to know I would be starting school the next day. I have always had a social personality and I was looking forward to meeting new friends. On the first day of school I was shocked at how large it appeared. Keep in mind, I had moved from a small farming town where my kindergarten class consisted of five students. As I arrived at this school it appeared to have a *million* kids running around.

As I went into my homeroom class I was happy to see that there were fewer kids, but still 10 more then I remembered having in my last homeroom class. The teacher was a tall older lady with small round glasses. She introduced herself to me as Mrs. Collins and held my hand as we walked to the front of the classroom. She then introduced me to the class and I felt a little shy as all of these small eyes were looking right at me. I was relieved when the introduction was over and a pretty little Hispanic girl with long black hair quickly walked up to me and asked me to be her friend.

Of course I smiled and said, "Yes! But....what is your name?"

She giggled as she replied, "It is Francesca, but everyone calls me 'Panch'."

The two of us then moved to the back of what appeared to be the longest line I had ever seen. Panch informed me that the teacher would give us all graham crackers and milk right before our nap time. I had never eaten graham crackers and milk before, but I knew it was going to be delicious! I watched as Panch dipped her graham cracker into her milk and I decided I would do the same. After the first bite, I thought I was in heaven!

As I laid down on the mat that had been assigned to me for my nap, I closed my eyes tightly and began to say a little prayer. I thanked God for the amazing graham crackers and milk and for my new best friend. I felt blessed and very happy with the new move.

Unfortunately, reality can hit at any age and it hit me hard the next morning when I arrived at the school. As I stepped off the bus that morning there was the most amazing smell coming from the school's cafeteria. As I came closer to the cafeteria door I discovered the smell was that of fresh baked blueberry muffins. I was excited to taste one! I thought to myself, "This school is amazing, not only do we have graham crackers and milk before our nap, but now we have blueberry muffins before school even starts!"

As I began to walk through the cafeteria doors I was quickly stopped by an older lady asking me for my ticket. I replied, "I am new, I don't have a ticket." She looked up my name in a big notebook and informed me I had a "pink ticket" which meant I could only have lunch at the school. She then asked me to go back outside and wait for the morning bell. As I turned to leave, the boy behind me was making fun of me and my "pink ticket." He was telling his friends I was a "poor kid" and continued to mock me. I noticed he had a white ticket which must have meant he had enough money to have breakfast at the school.

I ran outside to the back corner of the school and sat by myself in the snow crying, full of humiliation and disappointment. I asked God, "Why do I have to be poor? What does poor even mean?" This is when I realized being poor meant riding in a truck that did not have much heat, or living in a home where you had to haul your drinking water or sleep in the living room to stay warm. Poor meant not being able to have a blueberry muffin like the other kids in school.

I then did what my mother taught me to do and I prayed. I prayed that God would help me not to be poor anymore. I prayed that someday I would have as many blueberry muffins as I wanted. As I spent this time with God I heard the bell ring and I knew it was time to move forward. I was not going to let that boy see me cry. I stood up, wiped my tears, and went into the school. I knew God heard my prayers and someday I would be eating the best blueberry muffin ever made.

CHAPTER 2

A Prayer for the "Lost Souls"

"God, please save and heal my Jennifer" were the words coming from a soft loving voice I knew I had heard many times before. As a strained to see the face looking back at me, many memories shuffled through my mind. Oh yes.....It was the voice of my great grandmother, Millie. "What was she doing here in this white room?" I thought to myself. I wanted to give her a hug, but once again I could not move. Then more memories shuffled through my mind. "When was the last time I had seen her?" My heart sank when that memory came back in my mind.... It was several months before, during my last visit to my childhood church. I had not returned to that church since.

"Move, Move" said the voice of a concerned woman. "We will need for you to leave the room, her oxygen is dropping!"

"Grandma! Mom! Please don't leave me!" was what I attempted to cry out, but once again no one could hear me.

My sight was blurry, but I could see strangers quickly coming in and out of the white room. I then felt a horrible sense of fear come over my body.

"Am I going to die? Is God punishing me for not returning to church with my grandmother?" Then silence.......

When my family moved to Walsenburg we became involved with a very small Pentecostal Church. My mother was raised Pentecostal, and even though my Father was raised Catholic, they felt compelled to raise their children to follow my mother's religious upbringing. I attended this Pentecostal church throughout my childhood. I enjoyed the small congregation that consisted of about 20 members on a busy Sunday. The congregation was mainly older women who were always happy to see our young faces come in the doors each Sunday; one of them was my Grandmother Millie. The church was very welcoming to my family, as they were aware of my mother's Pentecostal background.

As a family we stayed close to the church and deep in prayer. Many of the church members knew of our move and our difficult financial situation. Members of the church would pray for us often and the church became a place of refuge for me and my family.

As time went on, our lives slowly began to change as my father went into a tree wholesaling business that was becoming more and more profitable each year. It was not a lot of money, but it was enough to keep food on the table and our cozy home warm. We were all very thankful for the prayers from our church and I could see my family becoming closer and closer to God.

Even though I loved our little church I began to struggle with the judgmental undertone that I would see and feel from time to time. At our Pentecostal church everyone would wear their "Sunday's Best." This meant slacks and ties for the men and dresses for the women. The women also wore veils on their heads when they prayed and during church service. Most of the congregation didn't have a TV and said you were "of the world" if you owned one. I would often hear them talking about those "sinners" they would see around town, but many of those "sinners" seemed to be nice people to me. I would often think to myself, "We have a TV. I wear jeans outside of church. Does this mean I am one of those sinners?"

As I became older I was more and more confused and torn in my emotions when I attended my church each Sunday. I loved the congregation and was so thankful to them for all of their prayers during my family's difficult time, yet I felt disappointed in them when they would talk about non-church members in such a judgmental way. There were some services where the Pastor would talk about how Jesus walked amongst the "sinners" and showed mercy towards them. I would look around the church and wonder, "Are they hearing this? He is saying Jesus is love."

When I was 12 years old it became apparent to me that my congregation was not hearing the true message of Jesus's mercy. That Sunday there was a new couple that came into our church and sat in the very last pew. They were a very quiet couple who kept their heads down as if they were embarrassed. They both appeared to be very sad and looking for some type of comfort. The lady was wearing jeans and a short shirt which exposed some of her stomach. She had long blonde hair that was messy and she had a thick layer of make up on her face. The man was wearing a tank top with holes in his jeans and unlaced work boots.

No one in the church greeted the couple. I watched as many of the members of the congregation looked at them in complete disgust. As the service went on my heart became more and more saddened for our visitors. The Pastor preached that day about "lost souls" and kept looking right at the couple in the back pew. The focus of the sermon was mainly stating if you were not living by God's "rules" you were going to "Hell." There was no love in the Pastor's voice; he was very stern and was obviously trying to get his message across to the church's new visitors. I wanted to jump out of my seat and say, "Stop!" But I was only 12 years old and I knew no one would listen to me.

Once the preaching stopped I looked back to the last pew and saw that the couple was gone. I could only imagine how they felt. I thought to myself, "Here was a couple seeking God and what did we show them? What would Jesus have done?" Sadly, I knew the answers to my own questions.

As a church, we did not show them anything but rejection. I also believed Jesus would have sat right beside them with a welcoming hand and I knew we should have done the same. As I walked out of that church, I regretted not welcoming that couple. I prayed that God would guide them to a new church that would accept them. I also prayed for what I thought were truly the "lost souls" which was my congregation that I cared about so much. Lastly, I prayed that God would show me a church of love and one that truly followed the heart of Jesus.

CHAPTER 3

A Fight for Survival

"I'm losing control, I'm losing control!" BANG!

I quickly attempted to open my eyes again as my heart appeared to be beating out of my chest.

"Was that a dream?" I thought to myself.

I tried to shuffle memories in my mind once again, but I had no recollection of a car accident. I kept thinking of my dream and how it felt so real. There had to be some connection between that dream and my current situation......

Although I do not remember the details, on June 12, 1994, my life would change forever on my way to work that sunny day. I remember saying goodbye to my parents as they left to watch an early showing of the new Flintstone's movie with some friends in a town that was 40 miles north of our home.

I felt a sense of excitement that morning knowing that my parents had left me the new car to drive to work that day. It was a white two-door Buick Regal which could go at a much faster speed than any of our other vehicles. It was also the first brand new car that my parents had ever owned and the sportiest one as well.

As I looked out the window at the shiny new car, I lost track of time as I was struck by the thought of driving it to work that day. Suddenly I looked at the clock and noticed I was running late. I was a waitress at a local restaurant and the summer was our busiest time of the year so there was no room for tardiness.

I have a very vague memory of the events that occurred the rest of that day. It all feels like a dream. I vaguely remember getting into the new car and driving down the road. I then remember suddenly feeling as if I was losing control of the car. It appeared to me the car was starting to fishtail as my back wheel hit some loose gravel on the side of the road. I had no idea how to make it stop and the last thing I vaguely remember was an overwhelming sense of fear. Then nothing……

I have no recollection of the events that took place after the crash. Later I was told that my car hit a guardrail head on at a high speed. Due to the intense force of the impact, my car doors sprung open, and I was ejected out of the car.

One of our neighbors said they heard a large bang during that same time. The couple said it sounded like a bomb had went off close to their property. They then called the State Patrol office with their concerns. Mr. Velarde was the State Patrolman that responded to the call. Unfortunately, I knew Mr. Velarde very well as he had a son that was my older brother's age and they were best friends. He had watched me grow up and would often come to the restaurant that I worked at for his afternoon coffee. He was such a kind man and would always leave me a bigger tip than the price of his meal.

That day our paths did not cross at the restaurant as they usually did on Saturday afternoons. They crossed in a hayfield 10 feet away from my crashed car. He found me lying on my stomach in a Superman position. I was talking and was very scared, calling out to him "I can't move, help me, I can't move." Mr. Velarde did everything he could to help keep me calm, as I cried out for help and began to struggle for each breath. The ambulance soon arrived and paramedics worked quickly to save my life.

I had broken my back, neck, and my rib cage was crushed penetrating my lungs which were quickly filling with blood and fluid. I was taken to our local hospital and was then sent on a Flight for Life helicopter to St. Frances Medical Center in Colorado Springs, Colorado.

Somehow I was able to tell the paramedics which movie theater my parents were going to that afternoon. My parents later described the sinking feeling they felt when they saw a police officer coming down the aisle of the movie theater calling for "Mr. Aguirre." My father stood up and said, "That is me." The police officer then escorted my parents to the lobby and asked them if they had a daughter by the name of "Jennifer Aguirre". After my parents confirmed they did have a daughter by that name, the officer then proceeded to explain I had been in a serious accident.

My father was in denial as they had just seen me only hours earlier. There was another girl in my hometown that had my same name and was only a year younger than me. My father insisted that the injured person had to be that girl. There was no way in his mind it could have been me. As the police officer went on to give details of the car, and the location of the accident, it became apparent that I *was* the injured person and my father was then silent with fear.

The police officer handed my father a phone. He listened closely as the physician at the local hospital I had initially been sent to, described my condition. My father was a large and very strong man, but this tragic news left him weak in the knees and fighting to stand. As my mother watched my father's body started to collapse and she knew something was seriously wrong.

When he hung up the phone all my mother could bear to ask was, "Is she alive?"

My father answered, "They say she is for now."

My parents were then quickly escorted to St. Frances Medical Center by the police officer. My mother described the trip as the most terrifying trip of her life. They did not know what to expect when they arrived. Their biggest fear was that I might not survive the helicopter ride. My parents arrived at the hospital and anxiously awaited my arrival. As the Flight for Life helicopter landed, the medical staff informed my parents I was still alive, but I had to be stabilized quickly. Due to the fact that time was critical to my survival, my parents were told they could only see me briefly as they brought me through the emergency doors.

Suddenly the doors flew open and there I was lying on a stretcher with several medical staff surrounding me. They all paused for a moment as my father reached out to grab my hand.

At that time my father said, "Jennifer?"

I attempted to open my eyes.

He leaned down close to my face as he whispered, "There are those pretty eyes."

I was then quickly whisked away by the medical staff caring for me. In that brief moment it was a relief to my parents to know I was still alive and I appeared to be somewhat responsive.

Through all of the initial shock, pain, and fear, my parents leaned on the one they knew had the control and that was God. They sat anxiously in the waiting room praying together as the medical staff worked to stabilize me. Finally, my attending physician entered into the waiting room and asked to speak with my parents privately.

The physician slowly escorted my parents into a small room were my x-ray results were hanging on the wall. In a very serious and steady voice he began to explain that I could no longer breathe on my own and I had been placed on life support for that reason. At that point he was very concerned that my vital organs were not going to be able to withstand the injuries even with the help of the life support. He then showed my parents an x-ray of my back and neck. He explained that my spinal cord had been severely damaged and surgery would be required to stabilize my injuries. He went on to explain I was not medically stable to undergo any type of surgery at that time. In that moment he was uncertain whether or not I would even survive.

My mother described the conversation as knives stabbing her in her stomach time and time again. The final stabbing pain came when the physician said,

"Even if she does survive, she will NEVER walk again."

My parents were then allowed to see me for the first time since I arrived at the hospital. When they walked into the room my parents experienced a horrifying feeling of fear as I appeared to already be dead. I was unrecognizable due to all of the swelling in my face. I could not squeeze their hands or look at them directly. My life support machine was the only thing creating any type of movement in my body, as it made my chest move up and down. The room was filled with beeping alarms attached to several machines. My parents stood silently in my hospital room, trying to comprehend all of the information that had just been given to them as they stared at their only daughter who was now fighting to stay alive.

CHAPTER 4

The Prayer that Saved My Life

For the first week I was placed in a large room in the ICU wing where I remained on life support and closely monitored. My face was so severely swollen that my eyes were almost closed completely. My body was black and blue from all the bruising and now I appeared non-responsive. I was placed on a flat rotating bed where I was completely restrained. The restraints were to ensure that my body would not move as the bed rotated completely from side to side. To my family this looked like some kind of torture device, but the nurses explained that the beds were used to prevent any further pulmonary complications.

It was hard for my family to understand all the tubes, alarms, and constant streams of medical staff coming in and out of my room. Though the nursing staff were kind, and did everything they could to explain each treatment, what appeared to be constant chaos did not bring my family any type of comfort or reassurance.

The first week passed very slowly and my condition did not appear to be improving. I was still on life support and there were no signs that I was going to start breathing on my own anytime soon. There were a lot of questions about my brain activity during that week. Was I responsive? Did I know where I was and what had happened to me? These were all questions my family continuously asked the medical staff. Unfortunately, I was the only one who could answer these questions….

Though I didn't know where I was, I could slightly see and fully hear most conversations. I remember straining to see my family as they came close to my bed and feeling hurt and confused as I saw the sadness on their faces. I also remember all of the alarms going off and the nursing staff talking to me as they came in the room. Most of all, I remember rotating side to side and wondering why I was not falling out of the bed.

Though everything seemed like a blur, there was one memory that will stay in my mind for the rest of my life. Actually, it still feels like it was yesterday when my attending physician came into my hospital room to speak with my parents about my medical condition. Though I could not see the man, I clearly heard his deep voice as he asked to speak with my parents alone in my room, of course not realizing I could hear every word he was about to say.

The physician explained to my parents that my medical condition was not improving and at that time there was no guarantee I would ever be able to breathe on my own. The physician went on to explain that even if I did survive there was no way to determine what kind of brain function I would have and what kind of quality of life I would live.

I strained to listen as closely as possible as my bed was rotating side to side. There were times I could see the three of them standing by the door and then my bed would rotate to the window.

As my bed was rotating back to where I could see them again, I heard the physician say,

"I recommend you stop the life support. She may survive a few days after that."

I could still hear my mother's cry as I watched her place her face in her hands. I had no way to tell them I was alert and I could understand every word. I wanted to beg them not to give up on me, but I could not make a sound.

I soon heard the footsteps of each one of them leaving my room and there I remained in complete silence.....

I knew in my heart that my parents would not stop my life support, but I needed to somehow show them a sign. I truly needed a miracle and I knew who to ask for one. Even though I was only 16 years old, I knew my relationship with God was strong and I believed He could hear me when no one else could. I also believed God could save my life even when the physician did not believe my survival was possible.

At that time I went into the deepest prayer with God I had ever experienced. I remember slowly closing my eyes and beginning to pray as my bed rotated towards the window of my hospital room. I asked God to save my life and I promised no matter what I had to face moving forward I would accept it knowing that he had mercy on me. As I opened my eyes again, I was overcome with hope as I saw a white bird land outside of my hospital room window. I knew this was a sign from God that he had heard my prayer. I believed God was going to save my life and I would have an amazing testimony to share with others.

CHAPTER 5

When Two or More Pray Together

Thankfully my parents refused to stop my life support and within days of my prayer to God, I began to breathe on my own. My ventilator was soon stopped and my road to recovery was looking brighter.

Many family members and friends arrived shortly after my flight landed at the hospital to show support and comfort to my parents. I was raised is a very small town with a great sense of community. Needless to say, word spread quickly of my car accident and soon many people were making the 90-minute drive each day. Many of those who came to show their support would sit in the waiting room with my parents, day after day praying for my survival. Most of them would never be able to visit me in my hospital room, but it didn't matter to them.... They would come anyway.

Between all of my friends and family I never spent a moment alone in my hospital room as they would take turns staying with me. I remember my mother greeting me as my bed rotated side to side. She would have to step up on a platform which was placed next to each side of my bed and would talk to me as the bed rotated from side to side. I have no idea how many steps my mother took a day, but her dedication to my healing was remarkable. It was also very comforting when I would look over at night and see my loving grandmother, Clara, sleeping in the chair next to my rotating bed with her pink sponge curlers in her hair. I knew she loved me as much as I loved her.

It was great to have so much support, but when the 4th of July rolled around that year there was an empty feeling in my hospital room and in the waiting room. All of our friends and family had returned home for the holiday and the only people who remained were my parents, my two brothers and our close friend named Matt. I believe the visitors helped to keep all of our minds off of the current situation and now the silence was a reminder of the tragic events that had happened and the challenges that still remained. God must have known we all needed to be uplifted and I believe He sent one of his angels to speak with my family and me later that evening.

This angel was a handsome black man that came into my hospital room and introduced himself as a housekeeper. When he saw my Bible by the side of my bed he said, "God is the only way."

Our newly-found angel went on to talk about the greatness and power of God. He had such an uplifting spirit that everyone in that room began to smile and regain a sense of happiness. He then looked at me and pointed to my body as I laid in my hospital bed. He confidently said, "It is already done, God has already healed her." He then smiled and left my room. We never saw that man again, as my family and I were hoping he would return. I truly believe God sent us an angel that day to lift our spirits and provide us the strength we needed at that moment.....

Once the holiday weekend was over the flood of loved ones returned to the waiting room and we soon learned there were now hundreds of people praying for my recovery. There is no doubt in my mind that the prayers from my friends, family and my community were what kept me alive during that time. The commitment, love and faith they all displayed, is something I will always remember and will forever appreciate! In the book of Matthew 18:20 (NKJV) the scripture states, "For where two or three are gathered together in My name, I am there in the midst of them." I know God was in the midst of that waiting room day after day and He HEARD the numerous prayers from each faith-filled person.

CHAPTER 6

My Prayer of Commitment Now Tested

As the prayers continued to flow, and my body continued to heal, I was eventually found stable enough to undergo an eight-hour surgery to stabilize my back and neck. My fractures were at the T5 level which is right at middle of the chest and the C3 level which is in the middle of the neck. Not only did these vertebras need to be stabilized, but Harrington rods where to be placed on both sides of my back to assist with my healing and posture.

That day the waiting room was once again filled with people praying for me during my surgery. My family had also learned that every church in my local community had started a prayer chain for me during this time. Thanks to all of these prayers my surgery went well and I was one step closer to recovery.

As the days went on, I became more and more alert. I began to notice there was something very different with my body. I would watch as the nurses would lift my legs, but I could not feel their hands. I would try to move my body, but nothing seemed to happen. I would think to myself, "Are there straps holding me down or have I lost my ability to move?" As weeks passed by it became more apparent to me that I did not have the ability to move my body, but why? It was the elephant in the room, and no one knew how to even start to discuss my injury with me.....

After being in the ICU for over six weeks my physician came in my hospital room and said, "You made it! You are truly my miracle patient!"

He went on to explain I would be having what is called a "halo" placed on my body to stabilize my back and neck the next morning. He then said I would be transferred out of the ICU and to a medical unit. I had no idea what a halo was, but it appeared fitting given my current situation and my miracle recovery.

The next morning my favorite nurse, Mabel, had me up early, giving me a bed bath before my halo was placed and I was transferred to my new hospital room. She was an excellent nurse and someone I had become very close to. She was kind, but stern. I had become very close to her as I knew when she was my nurse I felt safe and well cared-for.

That morning as she reached for my leg I asked her, "Why can't I feel you lift my leg?"

She quietly came to the head of my bed and said, "They have not told you yet have they?"

I said, "No, but you can tell me."

She moved my hospital gown to the side and said, "I am going to run my finger from your neck down. Tell me when you stop feeling."

As she moved her finger down the front of my body I stopped feeling right at my chest. My heart became very heavy as I realized this was more serious than I thought it was going to be. She explained that I was paralyzed from my chest down and the nerves in my left arm were also severally damaged. She said it would be impossible to know how much of my function I would ever regain.

She then said, "Only time and faith would tell."

It was such a sad moment for me. The first thing I thought was, "I will never ride a horse again." I then thought, "I will never dance again." I began to worry about how ugly I would be and how no one would ever want to date me. I looked over at Mabel and asked her for a mirror. I knew my body was damaged, but was my faced damaged as well? She was very hesitant to give me a mirror and at first she refused to do so. Once she reacted this way I was even more insistent and demanded to see a mirror.

As she placed the mirror in front of my face I was horrified to see what was looking back at me. All I saw was what looked like a monster! It had been over six weeks since my accident and my face was still very swollen and very black and blue. My hair was shaved off and I had several stiches that started at the top of my head and ended at the middle of my forehead. I looked like a bad mix of a boxer at the losing end of 12 rounds and Frankenstein in my mind. I had always taken pride in my appearance. I was 16 years old and of course at that age you think looks are everything.

Mabel sat with me as I shed many tears, but then she provided me with the most amazing words of encouragement. She explained to me that my face would heal and I would return to my normal appearance again. She then went on to say how she had taken care of many patients just like me who had lived rewarding and amazing lives as paralyzed individuals. Finally, she told me there was something special about me and she also believed my life had been saved for a purpose.

Then in true Mabel fashion she said, "Now let's get moving; you are getting out of here today and we don't have time for all this crying stuff."

I loved Mabel for the stern part of her as well as the caring part. I will never know if those are words that she shares with each discouraged patient, but I trusted her and in turn I believed her.

As Mabel and I shared this moment together we were soon interrupted as my physician came blazing into my hospital room holding a large medical device that looked like a cage.

He loudly said, "This is your halo, let's get it on you."

"What? Can we wait for my parents to get here?" I said fearfully.

"No time for all that." He said seriously as he looked directly at me.

My grandmother, Clara, had just walked back into my hospital room as my physician was assembling the cage-like device. She still had her pink sponge curlers in her hair, but it did not appear to distract him. He then turned to her and began to explain what he was going to do next as she stood nervously listening. He then quickly pulled out a tray with the biggest needles I had ever seen in my life.

As Mabel held my hand he injected my head four times, circling the top part of my skull. My grandmother's eyes were getting bigger and bigger, which was causing everyone in the room to become distracted. My physician then leaned over and pulled out some paperwork from the halo box. In a stern voice he directed her to move to the corner of the room and start reading.

My head quickly became numb, so numb I could no longer blink my eyes. He then placed the cage around my head and with a large drill-looking device he screwed the four parts of the halo directly into my skull one by one. I watched as my grandmother would poke her face around the side of the papers and grimace with every turn of the drill.

After he was done, I asked everyone to leave my hospital room. As I sat in my bed it took me a while to regroup from all of the emotions that occurred that morning. I had learned I was paralyzed, I had seen my monster-looking face for the first time, and now my head was screwed into some kind of cage. If this was the road to recovery, I was thinking twice about jumping on it. I began to cry and ask God over and over, "Why me?"

Even though my Faith in God was strong I slipped into somewhat of a depression after that day. I knew God had saved my life for a purpose, but how was *this* part of that purpose? Unfortunately, it became harder and harder for me to see God's vision for my life during that difficult time.

CHAPTER 7

The Impossible Becomes Possible

After two months of lying in a halo on the medical unit at St. Francis Medical Center I was on my way to the next step in my recovery and that was in-patient rehabilitation. After feeling sorry for myself during that time, I felt a new sense of excitement about my new journey. I was told this would be the place where I would be fitted for my new wheelchair and I would learn how to care for myself. This was exciting to me, as part of my depression was due to the fact that I had to rely on everyone to care for me. I had always been a very independent girl so the thought of becoming as independent as possible lit a new light in my fire.

My first day at the rehabilitation unit was an exhilarating one as I sat up in a wheelchair and began to roll around for the first time. I remember my family watching me as I pushed my wheelchair down the hall

and turned the corner to come back to greet them. were all overjoyed and filled with happiness. Thougl my surprise, pushing the wheelchair was a lot harder t I expected. I quickly became tired and my time in new wheelchair ended way too soon.

As time went on I began to realize how weak I was and unfortunately my depression began to s again.....

The depression seemed to increase each day attended my therapy sessions. Even though I had some feeling and movement back in my left arm, still significantly weak. On top of that, I had los my core strength so when I would sit on the edge bed I would just fall over. I had no sense of balan and it was very scary. Due to my weakness and balance, dressing and bathing was very difficult. take me 30 minutes just to get dressed. I never wo dreamed I would fall over trying to put my s shoes on. Not only was it frustrating, it was emb I truly felt disabled and it devastated me.

After my first couple of weeks of rehabilitati to pray at night that I would not wake up in th and I would frequently cry myself to sleep. every day getting easier, every day became h I was burned out with the struggles of my n wheelchair. I would plead to God telling Hin sorry, but I was not strong enough to fulfill I for my life. Even though I would cry and p ach night, nothing was changing. To my dis vould still wake up each morning......

One day a friend of mine brought me a book and it was about angels visiting patients that were in the hospital. I read it one night and I asked God to give me a sign, whether it was in a form of an angel or not I needed to know he was still with me.

My sign came in a form of a nurse that started her first shift that night. Her name was Jennifer as well and she was the most positive person I had ever met. She was in her early twenties and right out of nursing school. Jennifer was close to my age and I felt she could truly relate to what I was going through. Each night instead of pleading to God that I wouldn't wake up, I found myself talking to Jennifer. She made me feel human again and helped me to realize life was still worth living.

One night Jennifer told me she thought I was a good listener and that I should look into going to college as a medical social worker. She believed it would give me the opportunity to help others that had injuries like mine. I had never planned on going to college. In school I was more of the social butterfly and never was the one known for completing my homework. But Jennifer convinced me this was a start to my new life and I could go to college f I desired.

Jennifer made me feel like the sky was the limit for ne at a time that I really needed an angel. This is wher realized God may have not answered my prayers, le still heard them. Instead of answering my pra ie, God provided me exactly what I needed as HOPE.

After six weeks on the rehabilitati scharged home to my loving family.

strength in my left arm and sensation to my knees. Even though I had regained quite a bit of feeling, I still was unable to move my muscles from my chest down which remained a challenge. I was scheduled to continue therapy on an outpatient basis and I understood my recovery would remain ongoing.

Most importantly, I had finally come to a place of acceptance with my spinal cord injury and I found peace with my new body. I was ready to move forward and that started with returning to high school. I am proud to say that same year I graduated from high school and started college pursuing a Bachelor's Degree in Social Work. I felt very accomplished as I was able to live on campus on my own and I learned how to drive again with hand controls.

Four years later I graduated with my Bachelor's Degree in Social Work. I felt such a sense of achievement as I received my diploma during that graduation ceremony. I remember looking up in the crowd and seeing my loving nurse, Jennifer, standing next to my family and friends. They were all cheering me on as I rolled down the aisle. I remember thinking this was not only for me, but it was for them as well. Each one of those amazing people had stuck by my side through so much tragedy and now we were all "rolling" to victory together knowing that God had made the impossible....POSIBBLE.

CHAPTER 8

God, Forgive Me As I Have Failed You

Shortly after graduation I began working as a Medical Social Worker at St-Mary Corwin Hospital in Pueblo, Colorado. As I drove myself to my first day of work, I could not stop smiling. I thanked God for my new job and I prayed that He would help me to make good decisions that day. I never felt so close to God as that morning when I opened my car door and smelled the amazing smell of blueberry muffins. As I looked to my right I realized the hospital cafeteria was located right next to the employee parking lot. It took me right back to the morning of my childhood when I could not afford a blueberry muffin. Now, God had blessed me with the ability to buy as many blueberry muffins as I wanted.

I quickly transferred into my chair and made my way to the cafeteria. There on the counter were the most delicious-looking blueberry muffins I had ever seen in my life. Not only did I buy one, I bought two. As I sat in the cafeteria eating my blueberry muffin breakfast I knew God had once again sent me a sign that he was with me and he had heard my prayers years ago outside of my elementary school.....

After my first day of work, the next 10 years seemed to pass by very quickly. I am embarrassed to say I had moved further and further away from God as the years went on.

I was offered a management position at the hospital, but I was told I could only have the position if I obtained a Master's Degree in Business Administration. I found myself working two jobs, going to school during the weekend, and completing my homework at night. With my busy schedule I was spending less and less time attending church or reading my Bible. If I could say I had any kind of regret, it would be not including God in my life during this time. Unfortunately, the decisions I had made without God's guidance during those 10 years eventually began to catch up with me.

It all started in my early twenties when I married a man that I had dated since my senior year of high school and all through college. When he proposed after our college graduation it appeared the right thing to do was to get married. I never prayed for God's guidance before or during our marriage and from day one we had marital struggles. Our struggles started with our inability to agree on our own religious beliefs. He was raised Catholic and I was attending a non-denomination church. He refused to attend any church service unless it was a Catholic service.

Needless to say, we rarely attended church and God was not placed in the forefront of our lives.

I honestly regret not standing up for what I believed and for giving in so easily. He did not pray much, so I stopped praying. He was not interested in reading the Bible so I didn't read it either. Between our busy lives, and the lack of prayer, our marriage was anything but a marriage. We became more like room-mates instead of husband and wife. He was so focused on the next fancy car we could buy and I was so focused on my career that we lost sight of what really mattered, and that was God.

As we grew further and further apart I felt a great deal of emptiness in my heart. I knew God was tugging on my spirit and I felt I needed to listen to Him. I suggested to my husband that we should attend church that Sunday. I did not care if it was a Catholic or non-denominational church. All I knew was that God was calling me back to Him. My husband was not willing to attend church with me that Sunday so I decided to attend on my own.

As I sat in the church I felt so low and unworthy to even be in the presence of God. I had spent the past 10 years of my life focusing on what I wanted instead of what God had planned for my life. I kept thinking of my car accident and all of the prayers He had answered for me. God saved my life and here I was living a life without Him!

As I sat in that Catholic Church that day I asked God for forgiveness and I prayed that He would provide guidance for my marriage and my life moving forward. As the church service ended the Father of the church came up to me and placed his hand on my shoulder as he had seen my tears. He then kindly said, "God is with you and He will never leave you."

As I drove home that day those words kept echoing in my mind. I continued to pray that God would provide me guidance and reveal to me what I needed to do moving forward......

As time went on God did reveal many things to me about my marriage and I knew it was best for me to leave the situation. The day I decided to end my marriage I had no idea where I was going as I was franticly driving down the road. It was one of the most difficult decisions I would ever have to make as I did not know where I would live or what I was going to do next. I was so emotionally distraught that I found myself sitting outside of a McDonald's parking lot desperately praying to God for help. That is when I decided to call two of my closest friends in my life for help, Tom and Kathy Kelley.

I had worked with Kathy several years before and we stayed very good friends. Tom had quickly become like a father figure to me. Kathy and Tom were the type of people that would always love you whether you saw them every day or once a year. That night when I called Kathy for help I could hear the shock in her voice. I had never shared with anyone that my marriage was having problems and I was not the type of person that would breakdown in front of other people. When Kathy and Tom arrived I was so upset that I could not even drive. Tom drove my car to their home and I rode with Kathy and began to share the entire story with her.

Kathy and Tom provided me with so much love and comfort when I felt so much hurt, fear and loneliness. In a time when I found myself homeless, my dear friends opened their home to me for as long as I needed. Once again God had answered my prayers and placed more guardian angels in my path even after years of unfaithfulness.

CHAPTER 9

A Prayer for a New Beginning

During the next six months I lived with Kathy and Tom and experienced a flood of emotions. Going through a divorce is not easy, but through the chaos I found myself getting closer and closer to God. I was attending church on Sundays and remained deep in prayer. With every bad thing that would happen during the day I would find myself comforted by my loving friends.

Tom, Kathy and I spent many evenings sitting at dinner talking about life. One night I was surprised to learn Kathy did not know God. She said she believed in something, but never thought much about it after that. Tom was raised Catholic, but found himself somewhat distant from God. I was honestly shocked as I discovered this about my loving friends. Sitting beside me were the two most Christ-like people I had ever met. I began to pray that Kathy would find a relationship with the

God of love that I knew and that Tom would renew his relationship with God somehow, someday.

During the time I lived with Kathy and Tom my life would take another unexpected turn, but this time my job was being impacted. One morning while I was at work I learned the CEO of the hospital where I worked was *No longer with the Company*. This was devastating to me as he was a mentor of mine and had given me many opportunities throughout my career.

After this announcement, discussions began about changes that may occur within the hospital. One of those discussions focused on my departments. I was the Director of Post-Acute Care at the time and I supervised the skilled nursing unit, the in-patient rehabilitation unit, as well as in-patient and out-patient therapy services. The discussions suggested that some of my departments might be closed down or contracted out. The big question was.... With these types of changes where did it leave me? Would I lose my job?

The next day was a Saturday and I found myself curled up in my bed. I would have never imagined my life turning out this way. I was going through an awful divorce, I had no home to call my own, I was living paycheck to paycheck, and now there was discussion that I might lose my job. As I remained curled up in my bed I felt like my heart was in the pit of my stomach. I thought to myself, "Just when I feel like I am pulling myself up, something comes and knocks me back down again." I then whispered, "God, I am not as strong as you think I am."

As I pondered these thoughts for a while longer, I became more and more discouraged. I decided I was just going to give up! I was going to apply for disability and live with Kathy and Tom for the rest of my life. Then I wouldn't have to worry about a job, a house.....life would be so much simpler. But once again, God had different plans.

I soon heard Kathy's voice as she came into my room. She said, "Are you going to stay in bed all day?"

I loved Kathy for her joking yet direct personality, but that morning I did not feel like smiling.

Kathy knew something was wrong. She leaned over my bed and said, "Get up, I made breakfast and it looks like you need to talk."

As I slowly made my way into the kitchen, I quickly learned Kathy had no intention of letting me feel sorry for myself. I explained to her what happened at work and how I felt discouraged. I didn't even get to the part of permanently living with her before she quickly cut me off. Kathy looked right at me and said, "You are one of the most amazing people I know and you are going to be just fine!"

She went on to tell me she believed I was going to be a successful person and that I would find the right man and marry again someday. There was no room for feeling sorry for myself or questioning my abilities that Saturday morning. I was moving forward and that was that. I guess God knew I needed that extra push and Kathy was the perfect person to deliver His message to me.

I heard God's message loud and clear. That Sunday I went to church and I fully laid down all of my worries at

God's feet. I committed to God that I would not worry about what happened with my job. I asked God to fully take control of my life and I prayed that God would bless my life with a *new beginning*. And that is when my life started to change……

CHAPTER 10

Another Miracle

"Hello Jen!" said a loud voice coming from the front of my office.

There stood Dr. John Wyatt, who was a physician I had worked with for several years at the hospital.

"Do you have a minute? I met someone you need to call!" Dr. Wyatt continued to say as he made his way into my office.

"Sure, come on in," I said as I chuckled to myself since he was already sitting in a chair in front of my desk.

"I met a man named Darby Brockett and you have to meet him!" Dr. Wyatt said with great enthusiasm.

I listened as he continued to explain he had sat by Darby on a recent flight to Oregon. Dr. Wyatt talked to me about how he had worked with Darby several years before at another rehabilitation hospital and how impressed he was with Darby's leadership style. He went on to share with me that Darby had now started his own company and was building rehabilitation hospitals throughout the Western United States.

Dr. Wyatt then said with a big smile, "I told him about you, you have to meet him."

At first I was confused and I asked him, "Why would you tell him about me?"

"He is looking for good people to be CEOs for the hospitals he is building. You would be perfect!" replied Dr. Wyatt.

At that time, I thought Dr. Wyatt had lost his mind. I explained to him I had never been a CEO and why in the world would this man even talk to me, much less hire me?

Dr. Wyatt then looked at me seriously and said, "Don't ever doubt your abilities, Jen. Just call him."

Dr. Wyatt then handed me Darby's business card as he patted me on my shoulder and left my office.

Even though I thought the idea was very far-fetched, the thought of calling Darby stayed pressing in my mind. Later that day I was speaking to a friend who was a physician recruiter, named Randy. I asked him if he had heard of this Darby Brockette or the Ernest Health Company he had started.

Randy said, "Oh Yes, I have!"

Randy went on to talk about what an amazing man Darby was and what a high quality company he was growing.

Out of the blue Randy said, "Would you like me to set up a call with him for you?"

I was shocked, yet intrigued. I quickly found myself saying, "Yes!"

Soon after my conversation with Randy I was on a phone call with Darby. Our call went well, I quickly felt I was talking to someone I had known for years. As our conversation ended, Darby said someone from his office would be contacting me and within a couple of days I received a call from his assistant, Sheryl. She explained to me that Darby was going to be in Colorado the next week and he wanted to meet with me in person. She did not call it a job interview, just a meeting with Darby. I was thrilled but yet I had no idea what to expect. I bought the nicest suit I had ever owned in my life and headed to Johnstown, Colorado, for my meeting.

As I came into the hospital I was greeted by Darby who to my surprise was wearing more of a business casual attire, with some nice looking cowboy boots, and a great big smile. I thought to myself, "This is the CEO of the company? He seems so normal and not like an executive at all." I found myself instantly comfortable as we did not go into any type of formal meeting like I had expected Darby wanted to show me around the hospital first a we talked causally as we strolled through the building was so impressed with his kind spirit and demeanor. talked to every employee in the hospital and treated t all the same. This was shocking to me since the of the company that I was currently working for knew the leadership team by their cost center numb would never walk around the hospitals much less the frontline staff.

As we made our way back to the administra he invited me into the current CEO's office all talked for a while. I was amazed by his co

to quality care as well as his commitment to the positive culture of the company. I felt everything he saying aligned exactly with my goals and dreams of how rehabilitation hospitals should be led. He then asked the current CEO to leave the office. I soon became very nervous. This was it, what was he going to ask me? Did I make a good impression? Did I say enough? Did I say too much?

This was all running through my mind when he looked at me and said, "Can you be mean?" I was honestly so surprised by the question, I didn't even answer. He then went on to explain how sometimes CEOs have to be mean and I appeared so sweet and soft spoken. I knew in my heart my answer to this question was going to be the deciding factor as to whether or not I would be invited to be on Darby's team.

I took a deep breath and I sat up as straight as I could in my chair. I looked at Darby directly in the eyes and said, "I did not get to where I am today without being a strong person. Yes, I can be mean when I need to be."

Darby leaned back in his chair as he said, "Well then, how would you like to be the Chief Operating Officer here at Northern Colorado Rehabilitation Hospital?"

I calmly said, "I would love to be."

Inside I was screaming with joy, I wanted so badly to jump out of my chair and hug that man. I still think to this day if I physically could have jumped out of my chair, I probably would have.

After I accepted the offer he asked for the Director of Human Resources to come into the office and Darby began to explain to him what he had offered me. The

Director then told Darby there was not a COO position in Ernest Health yet. He was not sure how to proceed since there was not even a job description for my review.

As I sat in that office I was in shock! Not only did Darby offer me a job, he just created one for me. I didn't think the situation could become any more surreal until Darby explained to me that I would be trained to hold the title of CEO some day in one of his hospitals. Meaning, I would have to be willing to move out of state if needed. I didn't even think twice, I quickly agreed to move if need be. I was so honored and thankful for the opportunity, it was one of the most memorable times of my life.

As a I left the hospital later that day I thanked Darby for the opportunity and assured him he would not regret hiring me. I transferred into my car and parked in a parking lot down the road from the hospital. I needed some time to process everything that had just happen. Most of all, I needed to spend time with God and truly thank Him for blessing me with *another miracle.*

CHAPTER 11

I Am Saved

When I returned home from my time with Darby I gave my 30-day notice at my job and I started looking for housing in Johnstown, Colorado. I was so excited to start my new life and when I spoke with my friends and family I let them know God had answered my prayers for a new beginning.

The last thing left to do was to face my biggest giant and that was finalizing my divorce. I had come to terms with the fact that I did not care any more about my previous house or any of my previous possessions. I met with my attorney and agreed to the terms my husband had presented, which left me with some debt and nothing to show for it. Several times my attorney questioned my decision, but I had prayed about it and I knew God was telling me to let it all go.

I now had to focus on moving and my finances which were stressful subjects. My divorce was very expensive and I was already living paycheck to paycheck. It was everything I could do to save up $2,400 for the first month's rent and the deposit on my new rental home in Johnston. I had enough money leftover to purchase a mattress with a metal frame, a small brown couch, a blue card table that I was going to use as a kitchen table, and finally a small TV. It was not much, but it was mine and I felt great!

The day I was to start my new position was the day of my final court date finalizing my divorce. That morning I arrived at the courthouse and saw my soon-to-be ex-husband for the last time. When I watched him walk in the door I immediately felt all the emotions creep up inside of me which I had learned to suppress over time. I was able to pull myself together as I agreed to all of the terms and I quickly left the courthouse. Even though that morning was hard I had faith that God was now leading my path. I had to remind myself that God was not the focus of that marriage and I would *never* make that mistake again.

When I arrived in Johnston later that afternoon I went straight to work and poured my heart into learning my new position. I spent a lot of time training with Dennis Shelby who was the CEO of the hospital at that time. Dennis was a very kind man and a strong Christian. God could not have chosen a better mentor for me.

One Sunday, Dennis and his wife, Judy, invited me to Timberline Church which was located in Fort Collins, Colorado. Pastor Dary Northrup gave the sermon that day and it deeply touched my heart. I knew at that moment I had found my new church. I began to attend church regularly at Timberline and became part of the women's Bible study group. God had not only opened a door for my career to grow, but also for my spirit to grow closer to Him as well.

One day when I was in church, a girl with purple hair, grunge clothing, and piercings everywhere sat in the chair right in front of me. At first I was surprised to see her, but I then became very hopeful that she would enjoy the service. I found myself taking quick glances at the girl as she listened to Pastor Dary's sermon. I could not tell if she liked what he was saying or not as she showed no emotion. At the end of the service I thought I would introduce myself to her, but Pastor Dary's path crossed hers before mine did.

I watched as Pastor Dary placed his hand on her shoulder and said, "Welcome! I am so happy to see you!" This young lady looked at him, her eyes filled with tears, and she fell into his arms. It was the most amazing sight I had ever seen. I was looking at a Pastor who truly loved someone for who they were, not showing any type of judgment.

That night while I was saying my evening prayers I thought about that girl and the church I attended during my childhood. I sadly thought to myself, "She would have never been accepted there." I then remembered my prayer to God as a child when the couple was not accepted by my congregation. I remember praying that God would lead me to a church of love and one that truly followed the heart of Jesus. In that moment I realized God answered my prayers by leading me to Timberline Church.....

As I continued to attend Timberline, I noticed Pastor Dary would always end his sermons with talking about being "Saved." He would explain that this meant truly giving your entire life to God and accepting Him as your Lord and Savior. Pastor Dary would then ask those who were ready to make this commitment to silently raise their hands with all eyes closed throughout the congregation. Time after time I would close my eyes and think to myself, "I already asked God to come into my life." I let time after time pass until one morning something in my heart told me differently.

Throughout my life I had prayed and asked God for guidance, but I had truly not asked Him to come into my life as my savior. As Pastor Dary ended his service that day I decided to raise my hand and make that commitment. I felt such a moment of peace as I believed God had revealed to me that He had led me to Timberline Church for that moment and for that specific purpose. It was a beautiful time in my life and I will forever be thankful to Pastor Dary and his commitment to serving God through Timberline Church.

CHAPTER 12

Many Blessings Found in the Desert

The next year in my new position went by quickly and I soon found myself having another interesting conversation with Darby. He needed a CEO in Prescott Valley, Arizona, and he was calling me to see if I was interested in the position. Darby explained I would have to be in Prescott Valley in two weeks and I would be given the title of Interim CEO for the first 90 days. It made sense to me that he wanted to see if I could be successful as a CEO before I was given the permanent title. I accepted my new position and by that weekend I was packing my bags to move to Arizona.

When I shared with my friends and family that I was leaving that next week to a town and a state I had never been to, not all of them were very agreeable. I could understand their concerns. I was a young single lady in a wheelchair going to a town where I knew no one. But for some reason I believed God had opened this door for me. I had been praying for this moment and here it was right in front of me......

During the last service I attended at Timberline Church, before leaving to Arizona, I sat outside of the building thanking God for all of my many blessings.

There I was, a 31 year-old young lady leaving to be the CEO of a hospital! It all seemed so surreal! Many thoughts and memories raced through my mind at that moment. I remembered my childhood where I was labeled a "poor kid" and how I longed for the other things children had at my age. I thought how no one in my high school would have ever seen me as the smart kid or the one most likely to succeed. My memories then led to the physician in my hospital room who recommended that my parents stop my life support and the fear that ran through my body thinking my life was going to end right then and there. My mind then flashed back to the 10 years of my life that I wasted not serving God and how it resulted in a failed marriage, but God still showed his mercy.

All of those events had led up to that very moment.....

As I was sitting outside of Timberline Church knowing that God had answered many of my prayers and had put amazing people in my life to help me along the way, I couldn't help but wonder what he had waiting for me in Arizona.

The next couple of days were busy. In only two weeks, I had to find a place to live, move, and start a new job. I believed this was going to be a blessed move due to the fact everything was falling into place so easily.

Unfortunately, when I arrived at the hospital that first day things began to take a turn for the worse.

I quickly discovered the leadership team was at odds, the main referring physician within the community was not pleased with the current care, and staff complaints came flooding into my office. I called my Leadership Team into the conference room to try to gain an understanding of the current situation, but the meeting turned into a bickering nightmare. On my way home that evening all I could do was cry. I had left my family, my friends and my church for what appeared to be a disaster.

Once I arrived at my home I began to pray for God's guidance. That is when God reminded me of my first conversation with Darby when he asked me if I could be "mean." I realized that it did not mean I had to go into work yelling and screaming. It meant I had to remain confident in myself and make the decisions needed even if they were difficult ones.

As I arrived at work the next morning I decided I would pray every day for my hospital before I even entered the doors. In my daily prayer I would ask God to provide me with the wisdom I needed to lead my leadership team. I would also pray that God would provide me with the staff I needed to ensure excellent care was given to each patient.

In the months to come, I had turned over half of my leadership team and several other staff members. I spent many long days at the hospital and had to make many difficult decisions. I am sure there were times former staff members thought I was "mean", but my decisions were necessary for the hospital to move in a positive direction.

After 90 days as Interim CEO, there was significant progress within the facility and I was promoted to the permanent CEO position at Mountain Valley Rehabilitation Hospital. During my time as CEO, the momentum continued as the hospital was ranked #1 in the company by my second year. The hospital continued to shine year after year as it was ranked in the top 10% in the Nation of Rehabilitation Hospitals. Even through all of the success I never stopped praying for my staff and our patients. I honestly feel there was a supernatural blessing on the facility coming directly from God hearing my daily prayers.

CHAPTER 13

A Specific Prayer

Even though I was having a great deal of success in my career I would still go home to an empty house. I began to miss companionship. I missed having someone to go with me to dinner, or to a movie. I missed having someone to talk to when I got home at night (even though my dog Roxy was a great listener). I would fill my loneliness with work and I soon found myself eating all three meals of the day in my office. This is when I realized I needed to get a life!

I went to church that Sunday and I prayed for a companion. I had heard several times in church to be specific, that God wanted us to pray in detail for what we needed. That day I prayed for a companion who was a believer like me, someone that I could go to church with, someone who I could read the Bible with and finally someone who would accept me and my wheelchair entirely. I was not sure if God was going to bless me with just a friend or husband, but I was not going to settle for anything less than for what I prayed.

The very next weekend I met my future husband, Dustin. He was a quiet soul, but also a caring one. He was a believer in God like me and was one of the most down-to-earth people I had ever met. It did not take me long to realize he was a very special person who truly loved me and never saw me as a person with a disability. This became evident to me when Dustin told me while we were together that there would never be a place he would go that I would not be able to join him. I thought his statement was kind, but impossible in all situations. To my surprise, Dustin would follow through on his promise, time and time again.

Dustin's promise was tested as we went to the movie theater together during one of our first dates. I was honestly speechless when he carried me to the top of the movie theater so I could have the best seat in the house right next to him. That was just the beginning! He then created an adult backpack to carry me in so we could go hiking together. Dustin carried me on his back to so many different places that I would have never been able to come close to in my wheelchair.

Time and time again, I would find myself strapped to the back of my Prince Charming. It was honestly any girl's fairytale dream that had come true. From the night we met each other, Dustin and I spent every moment we could together and it became clear to me that God had led me to my future husband……

As we dated, Dustin and I would find ourselves getting deep into conversation about our spiritual beliefs and we would stay up for hours talking about our relationship with God. We agreed on many things except for our beliefs regarding attending church. Dustin had shared with me several negative experiences he had while he attended different churches and he was not interested in attending any more. He felt he spent his time with God on his own and that was all he needed. I believed I needed a church family, but I had not found one during my time in Arizona. I began to pray for God's guidance as we were not attending church together and this was something I specifically prayed for in my prayer for a companion.

During one of Dustin's visits to see me in Prescott Valley he passed by a church called "Living Waters." He told me the name had caught his eye. He then looked over at me and said, "I really like that name, we should go there." I was excited to hear he wanted to go to church, but I had to have more information than just a name. Right then and there I looked up the number on my phone and I called for more information. The person that answered the phone that day was Pastor Chuck Ray. His voice was very inviting and during our conversation I learned he shared the same type of beliefs as Dustin and I.

The next Sunday we attended Living Waters Church and Dustin was in for a big surprise. I had been raised Pentecostal so when I saw the congregation raising their hands and jumping in the aisles as they praised God I was not startled, but Dustin appeared surprised. As the music continued a man in the front aisle began to speak

in tongues. Dustin became very quiet and I thought to myself "So much for attending church together." I assumed Dustin would think the people in the congregation were crazy as that had been my experience in the past with other people who were not familiar with this type of worship. But, as I looked over at Dustin I was surprised as he appeared interested. As Pastor Chuck started his sermon Dustin found himself even more intrigued and intently listened to his words.

At the end of the sermon, Pastor Chuck then did an altar call. Dustin and I watched as many people stood in front of the church receiving God's Holy Spirit as others spoke in tongues and praised God. For someone who had never seen anything like this, Dustin was very accepting and from that time forward we became a part of the Living Waters congregation.

That evening I was so excited about our new church, I decided to call my good friend, Kathy, to tell her about our experience. Kathy was very happy for me and was very pleased to hear the relationship between Dustin and I was becoming even stronger. I was surprised as I could hear Kathy talking more openly about God and her new-found relationship with Him. I almost dropped my phon when Kathy shared with me that she had started attendi a Cowboy Church and she was going to be baptized t summer. Kathy went on to say that Tom was attendin well and was even a church volunteer at the local Vete Nursing Home.

Since the time I lived with Kathy and Tom, prayed they would find a renewed relationship wi Not only had Dustin and I found a new churc

Kathy and Tom had found theirs as well. That evening I learned that an answer to a prayer may not come right away, but God still hears them, and He knows the best time to provide an answer.

CHAPTER 14

And She Said "YES!"

In the summer of 2012, I found myself in Moab, Utah, flying over the Canyonlands with the man I loved. Dustin had planned a summer vacation for the two of us that ended with a private airplane ride in Moab. I am originally from Colorado and he is originally from Wyoming, little did I know the Colorado River and the Wyoming Green River met in Moab. It is a sight that can only be seen from an airplane and is well known for the way the two rivers swirl together at the bottom of a canyon.

When Dustin told me were going to Moab I was excited, but I became less excited as I learned we were going to fly over the Canyonlands. I do not enjoy flying, especially in small planes, but before I knew it we were in the air. After a while I began to relax and I became glued to my camera. The Canyonlands were one of the most amazing sights I had ever seen. As we flew over the canyon where the two rivers meet, I became speechless. It was such a breathtaking sight to see.

I was busy taking pictures when Dustin said, "Jen I need to ask you something."

"Wait a minute, I don't want to miss this!" I said.

As I had my camera glued to my face Dustin then pushed a ring next to my side and said, "Will you marry me?"

I began to scream and I threw my camera in the air. The pilot was pointing to his headset and kept saying, "You are screaming, in our ears!"

It took me a moment to realize I was probably damaging their ears drums, but I was so excited I could not control myself.

I looked over at Dustin as he placed the ring on my finger and I said, "Yes!"

God had answered my prayer for a Christian companion and there I was flying over one of the most amazing places I had ever seen with the most amazing man I had ever met. That moment was even more confirmation for me that God *does* hear our prayers!

In the months to follow we talked about our future. Living in Arizona, we were far away from our families and we knew eventually we would want to be closer to home. We decided to move to Wyoming that fall. I found myself happy yet hurting all at the same time. I had found my soul-mate, but I was now going to leave everything I had worked so hard for in my career.

My next conversation with Darby was about moving again, but this time it was not for another Ernest Health adventure. Darby was very supportive as I told him I was resigning my position and told me I deserved to be happy. During my last week of employment with Ernest Health I attended a dinner where I said my farewells. During this time, Darby shared with everyone about our first meeting and how he asked me if I could be mean. His eyes filled with tears as he wished me the best and he said "Good Luck Kiddo", which was the nickname he had always affectionately called me.

From that meeting I flew to Wyoming and on September 16, 2012, I was married to the love of my life by Pastor Chuck Ray. This time I continuously prayed for God's guidance and there was no doubt in my mind that God would be in the forefront of our marriage.

CHAPTER 15

A Prayer for a Child

In the fall of 2012 Dustin and I said good-bye to our Arizona friends and moved to Alcova, Wyoming. We bought a home on the Alcova Reservoir which resulted in us living much closer to our family and close friends. As the holidays came near Dustin and I started to talk about having a family of our own. I had been told time and time again that I would have a higher risk of medical complications while giving birth due to the level of my spinal cord injury. Now I had reached the age of 35 which increased these risks, but I found myself wanting to have a child of my own.

I had never thought of being a mom until I met Dustin, but now it was something I greatly desired. I knew it was because I could tell Dustin would be as good of a father as he was a husband. There was something burning deep in my heart that made me want a child and the desire grew greater and greater. After a long conversation, Dustin and I decided having a child of our own would be worth the risk. We spent time in prayer together and asked God if it would be His will, I would get pregnant. If it was not God's will, I would not. It was as simple as that, so we thought.

I soon found myself praying desperately that I would become pregnant. Month after month my hopes of being pregnant would grow stronger and to my disappointment it was not happening for me. I purchased so many pregnancy tests during that time Dustin suggested we buy stock in the First Response Company. After three months of trying, I became discouraged and I started to accept that God must not want us to have a child. I remember sadly thinking "What is wrong with me? Maybe, I would not be a good mom?" I then decided that God knew best and I stopped focusing on getting pregnant......

In April of 2013, I woke up one Saturday feeling very tired and as if I was coming down with a cold. As the weekend progressed, I became more and more abnormally tired, but no other symptoms had developed. I had read in one of my *mommy to be* books that women feel very tired during their first term of pregnancy. I didn't want to excite myself, but I thought maybe there could be a chance I was pregnant.

On our way home from church that Sunday I asked Dustin to stop at the store and buy a pregnancy test for me. He rolled his eyes and said, "Really, I thought we were not worrying about this anymore." I made him purchase one anyway and as soon as we returned home I took the test. I waited anxiously and to my disappointment the test read, "NOT PREGNANT." My heart sank as I looked up at my loving husband who came over to me and held me tightly. He said, "It is really ok, we have each other and that is all that matters." I felt comforted, but still disappointed.

As the week went on I remained very tired, but I never developed any cold symptoms or anything that would indicate I was becoming ill. I began to think something else was medically wrong with me so I made an appointment with my physician, just to make sure nothing else was happening.

As we sat in the exam room all of my vital signs were normal and my physician explained she thought I was very healthy. She then said with a questioning look on her face, "Could you be pregnant?"

I told her we had been trying, but that I had recently taken a pregnancy test and it was negative. She insisted that I take another one in the office just to make sure. I reluctantly took the test, knowing it was going to be negative and I was not excited about feeling the disappointment again.

As Dustin and I sat in the exam room, my physician slowly opened the door, and entered the room. She had a perplexed look on her face which made my heart began to race. She sat next to me as she began to smile and said, "Congratulations! You are pregnant!"

I could not believe what she was saying, it was really happening! I then looked over at Dustin who appeared to be glowing as he said, "It's going to be a Waylon, I know it!"

I chuckled as he had been talking about the name Waylon before we were even married. My physician then explained she thought I was close to four weeks along and my due date would be December 18th. "Wow, a Christmas baby" I thought to myself. What a blessing that would be!

Dustin and I then raced to our car and sat in the parking lot as we called everyone we knew. I had honestly never been so happy in my life. I was going to have a child with a man I loved more than anything. It was a moment I never would have dreamed could happen to me, but through God's grace I was finally pregnant.

CHAPTER 16

My Biggest Accomplishment

For the next four months Dustin would sing to my tummy old Waylon Jennings and Johnny Cash songs. When someone would ask how the baby was coming along, Dustin would say, "Waylon was doing great!" I was worried that we were going to have a girl and Dustin would be disappointed. As I talked to him about my concern he convinced me that he would love a girl, but still had no doubt in his mind we were having a *Baby Waylon.*

When I was 20 weeks pregnant we went in for a special check-up. We had been waiting for this day for some time, since this was the day of our ultrasound where we would find out the sex of our baby. Dustin was so excited that morning. He had told me he knew this was going to be a great day since it was his mother's birthday. Dustin's mother had only passed away a couple of years prior and I knew he still missed her more than words could say. I could hear the sadness in his voice as he quietly said, "I sure wish she could be here." The mood quickly changed as we arrived at the physician's office.

I knew Dustin's mother, Barbara, was smiling down on us that day when our physician showed us the ultrasound and said, "You are having a BOY!"

I had such a sense of relief and happiness as I watched Dustin glow with excitement. For the rest of the day I listened as Dustin talked about everything he and Waylon were going to do together. I had never seen my wonderful husband so happy.

Unfortunately, I was not as happy or excited during most of my pregnancy. From the day I found out I was pregnant, until the day I gave birth, I had morning sickness 24/7. I also experienced every other symptom you could have during pregnancy. Instead of gaining weight, I was losing it. Every night I had to remind myself.....*you prayed for this!*

Even though the pregnancy was difficult, I was fortunate to have an excellent physician who took great care of me. But as my due date came closer, I could tell he was nervous about my delivery. He explained to me during one of my check-ups that 78% of women at my age, and with my type of spinal cord injury, had experienced a stroke while giving birth. After completing this research, he suggested that I have a Cesarean and recommended that I also have a physician group out of Denver that specialized in high-risk mothers follow my case. This information and recommendations made Dustin and I concerned.

But on our way home from our appointment that day, Dustin and I decided we were not going to let worry fill our hearts. We were going to continue to have faith in God and pray for a healthy baby and a safe delivery. We both knew God had allowed me to become pregnant and we believed there was no reason why He would allow anything to happen to either one of us......

To my surprise, the day before Halloween I woke up with a fever and as the day went on my body began to shake. I quickly made an appointment to see my physician and he diagnosed me with a urinary tract infection. He had me transferred from his office to the local hospital to have a Foley catheter inserted and ordered IV antibiotic treatments to be started. I thought I would spend one night in the hospital and then return home the next day.

Unfortunately, during the Foley catheter insertion I went into preterm labor. I was 32 weeks pregnant and the small local hospital I was at did not have the ability to care for that premature of a baby if I truly went into labor. The contractions were getting harder and harder and I was quickly flown to Presbyterian Medical Center in Denver, Colorado.

I will never forget that night as I was in that small plane with two pilots, two nurses and Dustin. As they explained to me what would happen if I had Waylon on the airplane, all I could do was close my eyes and pray for God's help. I had so much fear and I was very worried something would happen to my unborn child. As I opened my eyes, all I could see was snow hitting the windshield of the plane. I then realized we were flying in the middle of a blizzard and I became more and more fearful. With tears in my eyes I looked over at Dustin as he kept reassuring me everything was going to be just fine.

I praised God, when we finally landed at the hospital and the contractions had begun to subside. Baby Waylon couldn't wait to come into this world, but we were able to put him on hold for a little while longer.

I spent two weeks after that in the hospital on bed rest. The physicians informed us that Waylon's lungs would be fully developed by 34 weeks. Every night I would pray that Waylon would not come before the 34-week mark and once again God heard my prayers.

At 34 weeks and four days my water broke and our Baby Waylon was coming whether we were ready or not. I will never forget the moment as I looked at Dustin and said, "I think my water just broke!"

He looked at me and to my surprise he said with great excitement, "Do you know what today is? It's the Marine Corps Birthday!"

Dustin had served in the Marine Corps and had always celebrated this day as if it was one of the major holidays. He was so excited that he began to text message all of his Marine Corps buddies. I had to quickly remind him I was still in the room and Waylon still had not arrived yet.....The pressure was then on to have Baby Waylon by midnight!

Waylon Dean Crouse was born naturally on November 10, 2013, at 9:03 p.m. and he proudly now shares this special day with the United States Marine Corps. For a five-week premature baby he still weighted a solid five pounds and was 19 and ½ inches long. Waylon spent eight days in the Neonatal-ICU and every night Dustin would sing Waylon Jennings songs to him just like he did while he was in my tummy. I was amazed when Waylon would look right back at Dustin as if he already knew his daddy's voice. The bond that Dustin and Waylon instantly shared was such a remarkable sight to see.

Dustin and I were very proud parents as we took our little blessing home that next Monday morning and three months later Waylon was dedicated to God by our loving Pastor, Chuck Ray. Our prayers for a healthy baby had been answered and we had never felt so blessed.

CHAPTER 17

A Different Way to Pray

When Waylon was two months old Dustin had come down with Bronchitis and I found myself caring for a new baby on my own. After a week of no sleep, and complete exhaustion, I called my sister-in-law, Dawn, for help. When Dawn arrived that evening I shed tears of joys as she walked through our front door. During that time, I believed God had sent Dawn to help me care for Waylon. But later that week I realized God's true purpose for sending Dawn to our home.......

One night Dawn and I were talking in the living while Dustin and Waylon slept. As the evening went on, I suddenly felt an overwhelming tug on my spirit telling me to ask Dawn to pray for me. I had no idea why, but I asked her and she happily agreed.

Dawn and I moved closer to one another until we were sitting side-by-side on my sofa. Dawn held my hands tightly in hers as we both closed our eyes. She began to pray very slowly and quietly. I listened as she prayed that God would give me strength and discernment. Then, I felt a tingling feeling begin to move through my arms as she quietly began to pray for me in words I did not understand. I quickly could tell that my body had become filled with God's Holy Spirit. It was a supernatural feeling that was hard to explain, but I knew it was very real. After Dawn finished her prayer I felt exhausted, yet renewed.

I was aware Dawn had the gift of speaking in tongues and in that moment she was fully utilizing her gift. In the past, I had always had mixed feelings about the gift of tongues. Sometimes I was fearful and other times I had doubt whether or not it was even possible. But that night, as we prayed in my living room, I realized the gift of praying in tongues was real and it became apparent to me that Dawn was blessed with this amazing gift. I will never know the words that God had given to Dawn that night, but I knew God was using Dawn's prayers to prepare me for a new journey. It was a life changing moment for me in more ways than I will ever be able to comprehend.

CHAPTER 18

A Calling to Share My Story

After my time with Dawn, Dustin and I prayed for God to lead our path as I had a desire to return to work. I missed helping patients and leading a team. I prayed as Dustin fasted about this desire of mine. I then decided to give Darby a call. If I was going to return to work as a CEO I could only see myself working with my Ernest Health family.

When I called Darby he was happy to hear from me and he kindly said he still had my Christmas card sitting on his desk. He asked how Waylon was doing and he asked about Dustin. He still was the caring person I had grown to love and respect. I had expressed to him that I wanted to return if possible in whatever capacity he saw fit. He explained to me that he had become so busy with the growth of the company he handed over most of the hiring responsibilities to Tony Hernandez who was now the Vice President of Operations.

I later spoke with Tony who offered me a position as the CEO of Northern Utah Rehabilitation Hospital in South Ogden, Utah. I had been praying for this moment, but I was surprised the opportunity was in Utah. Dustin and I asked ourselves, "Why would God move us to Utah?" Even though we were not sure what God's plan was going to be for us, we decided to follow His lead and we moved to Utah.

Once we arrived in Utah the days became extremely busy. Starting a new hospital takes definitely more than a 40-hour work week and I was a full-time mommy when I returned home. Though we were busy, everything seemed to be coming together except for our journey to find a new church.

Dustin and I had been to several churches during our first four months in Utah, but none of them seemed to be the right fit. During a 4th of July celebration Dustin and I would find the answer to our prayer for a church family. That day we were attending a "breakfast in the park" celebration when we found ourselves with my wheelchair stuck in the grass and Waylon crying in his stroller. Dustin was trying to help both of us, but he was becoming more and more overwhelmed. Right then a very nice couple came up to us and they helped me with my wheelchair as Dustin cared for Waylon. We were both so thankful for the kind gesture.

Dustin and I were surprised when this nice lady looked at us and said, "You have just been ROCKED by the Genesis Project!" We looked at her very confused yet interested as she went on to explain she was a member of the Genesis Project Church in Ogden. She then kindly reached for my hand and asked if the two of them could pray for us. I the middle of hundreds of people the four of us stood praying with Waylon in the center. It was such a testimony to me of her faith in God. As we left the park that day, I looked over at Dustin and said, "I think we have found our Church."

That Sunday we attended the Genesis Project and it did "ROCK" as the nice lady expressed to us. We were so impressed with the sermon we stayed after to introduce ourselves to Pastor Matt Roberts. As we spoke with Pastor Matt we found him to be a very kind and inviting man. When he spoke, I could tell the love of Christ was in his heart. I instantly felt like I was talking to a friend and not a stranger. The church service reminded me so much of my time at Timberline and Pastor Matt displayed so many of the same characteristics of Pastor Dary.

During our conversation, all of the similarities began to make sense as we learned the Genesis Project was affiliated with Timberline Church and Pastor Matt knew Pastor Dary well. I was amazed that God had led us to the one church in Ogden, Utah, that was affiliated with the church I called home in Colorado. At that moment I realized that God was greater than I would ever be able to begin to comprehend……

As we continued attending the Genesis Project I felt a calling I had never felt before. It was an internal voice telling me that I needed to get more involved with our church. I felt this was the most powerful tug on my spirit I had ever experienced. Dustin and I decided to meet with Pastor Matt and tell him that we wanted to be more involved with the church in some way.

As we drove to our meeting with Pastor Matt we talked about the types of things he might want us to help with. Maybe he would ask us to pray with other people or feed the homeless. We both decided that daycare would not be our strength, as we chuckled, and smiled at each other. But to our surprise Pastor Matt asked us to be Bible study leaders at the next round of Bible study sessions. Of course we agreed, but once we sat in our car Dustin and I looked at each other and said, "Bible study leaders?" We had never led a Bible study and we were very nervous about it. But, we were the ones who had asked for God to guide us, so there we were on the path to Wednesday night Bible study.

To my surprise, our first night of Bible study was amazing! God had placed the most special people in our group and we all made a great connection. It was not until the second session that I realized why God had led us to be Bible study leaders…..

The topic for the study that evening was, "Do our lives even matter?" The Bible study was based on The Parable of the Talents from Matthew 25: 14-30, NKJV.

It reads:

> *14. "For the kingdom of heaven is like a man traveling to a far country, who called his own servants and delivered his goods to them. 15. And to one he gave five talents, to another two, and to another one, to each according to his own ability: and immediately he went on a*

journey. 16 Then he who had received the five talents went and traded with them, and made another five talents. 17 And likewise he who had received two gained two and more also. 18 But he who had received one went and dug in the ground, and hid his lord's money. 19 After a long time the lord of those servants came and settled accounts with them.

20 "So he who had received five talents came and brought five other talents, saying, 'Lord, You delivered to me five talents; look, I have gained five more talents besides them.' 21 His lord said to him, 'Well done, good and faithful servant; you were faithful over a few things, I will make you ruler over many things. Enter into the joy of your lord.' He also who had received two talents came and said, 'Lord, you delivered to me two talents; look, I have gained two more talents besides them.' 23 His lord said to him, 'Well done, good and faithful servant; you have been faithful of few things, I will make you a ruler over many things. Enter into the joy of your lord.'

24 "Then he who had received the one talent came and said, 'Lord, I knew you to be a hard man, reaping where you have not sown, and gathering where you have not scattered seed. 25 And I was afraid, and went and hid your talent in the ground. Look, there you have what is yours.'

> *26 "But his lord answered and said to him, 'You wicked and lazy servant, you knew that I reap where I have not sown, and gather where I have not scattered seed. 27 So you ought to have deposited my money with the bankers, and at my coming I would have received back my own with interest. 28 Therefore take the talent from him, and give it to him who has ten talents.*
>
> *29 'For to everyone who has, more will be given, and he will have abundance; but for him who does not have, even what he has will be taken away. 30 And cast the unprofitable servant into the outer darkness. There will be weeping and gnashing of teeth.'*

I had heard this parable several times before and it honestly made me fearful. It was not until that night God opened my eyes to the significance of the parable in my life. As I sat in my chair God revealed to me that I was the last man in the parable, the one who was hiding his talent which was my testimony.

I began to realize that God was telling me He had saved my life to share my testimony with others and I was not. It was so clear to me, I became speechless. I began to cry as I felt an overwhelming sense of guilt. In my heart I knew God was calling me to be more than a mom, more than a wife, more than a CEO. God was telling me to share my testimony of how He answered my prayer and saved my life when it was said to be impossible. Most importantly, God was calling me to share how He had continuously blessed me from that day forward!

As I read the parable again it became even clearer to me that God had called me to be His soldier, one that would use my gift to bring hope to those who were hurting, hope to broken families….HOPE to anyone who would be willing to listen to my testimony. It became apparent to me that God had saved my life for this purpose and it was now my responsibly to follow through with what He had called me to do.

CHAPTER 19

All Glory is His

I have learned throughout my life that when God is leading your path He will place people in your life that will help you along the way. This was the case, as Dustin and I were parked in our local mall when a beautiful lady pulled her car next to ours. I was surprised as I looked closer at the car and saw a mechanical lift in the back of the Subaru she was driving. The device then began to lift a wheelchair from the back of her car next to the driver side door. As Dustin and I watched she looked over at us and said in a very friendly voice, "Hello! Do you want to see how this lift works?" We began to engage in a conversation and quickly found ourselves exchanging information. Her name was Meg Johnson and I later learned she was the president and co-founder of the Ms. Wheelchair Utah Pageant.

I had never heard of a Ms. Wheelchair Pageant and I soon learned this was not just *any* pageant. In a later conversation with Meg she explained to me that it was not a beauty pageant, but a pageant that focused on advocating and inspiring others with disabilities. Meg encouraged me to apply and after some time in prayer I decide to do so. Two months later I was a contestant in the pageant and I was crowned Ms. Wheelchair Utah 2015.

I soon learned that my reign as Ms. Wheelchair Utah had nothing to do with wearing a crown. God had placed me in this spotlight to share my testimony at a much larger level. I soon found myself covered by the local news stations, on the radio, featured in the local paper, and speaking at different events. My testimony was quickly being shared on social media and my website was being viewed not only in the United States, but in several other countries as well.

I began to receive text messages, calls and emails informing me that my testimony had helped so many people. To my surprise, the individuals contacting me were not only those who were disabled, but many of them were able-bodied people who felt they had been touched by my message. I felt so humbled and inspired to keep marching forward as God's soldier, giving all glory to Him.

As part of holding this title, I was heading to Iowa in July for the Ms. Wheelchair America Pageant. I found myself feeling more and more competitive as the pageant came closer. I actually would feel guilty from time to time, telling myself it was not right to want to win the crown. When I arrived in Iowa, God and the 24 other women in the pageant would touch my heart and my desire to win quickly diminished.

The competition was a week-long with 25 states represented by the most amazing women I had ever met. During registration, I was given an itinerary that was very extensive. Each contestant would be interviewed by the judges three different times and when we were not in judging we would be attending educational sessions. During the evening we would attend dinners that had a fun theme which would give us all an opportunity to get to know each other better. The final two nights consisted of each contestant giving a speech about their platform. THEN…..The Final Crowning! As I read through the material I felt excited and ready for this adventure.

That night during our first dinner together each contestant told their stories and why they had chosen their platforms. At first I could not wait to share my story and platform. I have to admit, I was a little disappointed that I was going to be one of the last to speak since the facilitator was going in alphabetical order and I represented Utah.

My frame of mind changed once the women began to speak. I quickly became captivated by each of their platforms and personal stories. I found myself inspired and in tears with each presentation. I realized I was in the presence of such strength, determination and inspiration. When it was my turn to speak, each story had so greatly humbled me that my presentation was faster than I had planned. I found myself quickly returning to my table, eager to hear more about the other contestants and wanting to speak less about myself.

When I returned to the hotel room after dinner Dustin was up waiting for me. He was surprised as I sat in our hotel room and began to cry. I shared with him all of the stories I had heard that evening and described all of the amazing women I had met. I told Dustin it had became clear to me God did not send me to the pageant to win a title or a crown, He sent me there to experience this humbling moment and share my testimony along the way.

Day after day, I was able to get to know each contestant at a deeper level and night after night I was sharing their stories with Dustin in complete and total awe. I prayed each night that I would be able to make as much of a positive impact on each one of their lives as they were making on mine. On the night of our speeches I spoke about my platform which was "Accomplishing Your Dreams After An Injury." I was able to share my testimony at that time and how God had blessed my life. After my speech I prayed my story had touched at least one of the contestants in a positive way.

On the final night, all of the contestants lined up as we prepared to be called up on the stage state by state. We began to hold hands and it was a beautiful sight to see. Each one of us had come to a competition that had developed into a sisterhood. In that moment I closed my eyes and prayed that God would send His Holy Spirit through our arms and touch each one of our lives. As I stayed with my eyes closed, I had an image in my mind of the Spirit of God flowing through each contestant's hands, to their arms, into their bodies and then moving to the next contestant. As I continued to pray I knew God was running through our bodies and I could feel it!

As the pageant began, I felt so honored when I received the Lifetime Achievement Award which was awarded to the contestant that had a significant impact advocating for people with disabilities. Even though I did not win the crown that night, I had such a sense of humility and happiness. I was able to share my testimony with hundreds of people and God had been glorified!

CHAPTER 20

Nothing is a Coincidence

In the summer of 2011 I met a man by the name of Howard Skinner at a church service in Bird City, Kansas. He was a guest speaker in the small church we attended while visiting Dustin's family. Dustin and I could see the power of God radiating from Mr. Skinner and after his service I asked him to pray for Waylon and me, as I was six months pregnant.

Mr. Skinner prayed for me silently and then he said God had given him a message for me. He leaned over to me and said, "Your baby is going to be fine. You don't have to worry about that."

I smiled at him and then he said, "God also wants you to know He appreciates your testimony."

Mr. Skinner then hugged me tightly and walked away.

After this conversation I felt relieved yet confused. I was happy for the reassurance regarding Waylon, but what did he mean by "God appreciates my testimony?" What was God trying to tell me?

As we left the church that day Dustin purchased Mr. Skinner's book titled *Secrets to Our Supernatural Walk with God*. We began to read in Mr. Skinner's book of the many supernatural miracles he had experienced in his life. His testimony was encouraging and very inspiring. It quickly became clear to me he was a true man of God and had many gifts of the spirit.

It was not until recently, as I began to share my testimony, that I realized what God was saying to me through Mr. Skinner that Sunday. I believe God had already shown Mr. Skinner that He would open many doors for me to share my testimony with thousands of people and God was telling me that He appreciated my decision to follow His will.

That message from God and my entire life experience have led to *this* moment in time. It has led me to write this book and it has led *you* to read it. Just as God had placed many amazing people in my life, He is now touching your life for some reason through this book. It is not a coincidence that this book has crossed your path. I know from experience that God is tugging at your spirit just like He did to mine time and time again.

What is so beautiful about the Grace of God is that you don't have to be a perfect person, just one that is willing to make a change and a commitment to live your life for Him. As you have read in this book, time and time again I doubted, time and time again I failed, and returned to God. Each time I returned asking for forgiveness and recommitting my life to God.

As I became more committed to following the path God had set for me, and staying deep in prayer, God has elevated my life to a level I would had NEVER thought was possible. God took a poor, uneducated, disabled country girl and guided her to a path were she is now a Wife, Mother, CEO and an Advocate for others with disabilities. Only God can create this type of miracle which leads me to KNOW He is real!

There is no doubt in my mind that God can do the same for you as He has done for me. If you have doubt or are asking yourself how or when, I can tell you my friend, all it takes is time and a lot of faith. But if you start with a belief in God, and begin to pray with all your heart, He WILL hear your prayers.

I pray that this book is the PROOF you need to know God heard my prayers and will hear ***yours*** *as well*!

About the Author

Jennifer Crouse is a wife, mother, CEO of Northern Utah Rehabilitation Hospital, and was named Ms. Wheelchair Utah 2015.

At the age of sixteen, Jen was in a car accident that left her paralyzed from the chest down, and she was not expected to survive. By the grace of God, she did. After spending a week on life support, Jen prayed to God to save her life, and shortly after this prayer, she was able to breathe on her own. After being hospitalized for over four months, Jen returned home, and she was called a miracle by many of the physicians who cared for her.

After this accident, Jen knew her purpose in life was to help others by sharing her story of how through prayer God saved her life. Jen went on to earn a bachelor's degree in social work from Colorado State University and a master's degree in business administration with an emphasis in healthcare management from the University of Phoenix.

Jen now travels the country sharing her story of how God saved her life for a purpose and helps others to find their purpose as well.

Printed in the United States
By Bookmasters